ALL AMERICAN PATRIOTIC
SONGBOOK

Edited and Produced by John L. Haag

Voice ★ Piano ★ Guitar

Catalog #07-1004
ISBN 1-56922-035-2

CREATIVE CONCEPTS
P U B L I S H I N G

EXCLUSIVELY DISTRIBUTED BY
HAL•LEONARD®
CORPORATION
7777 W. BLUEMOUND RD. P.O. BOX 13819 MILWAUKEE, WI 53213

Visit Hal Leonard Online at
www.halleonard.com

ALL AMERICAN PATRIOTIC
SONGBOOK

ALEXANDER'S RAGTIME BAND
FROM "ALEXANDER'S RAGTIME BAND"

Words and Music by
IRVING BERLIN

Alabama Jubilee

Words by JACK YELLEN
Music by GEORGE COBB

America
(My Country Tis of Thee)

Words and Music by
Samuel F. Smith and Henry Carey

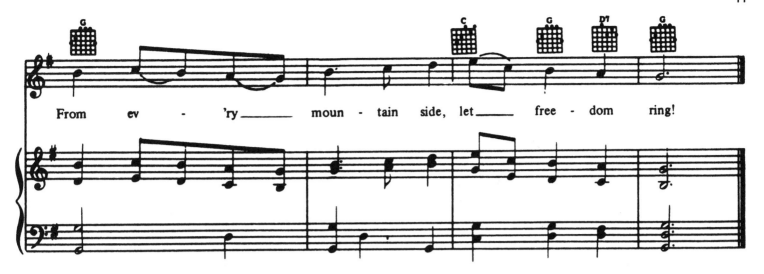

From ev - 'ry_____ moun - tain side, let_____ free - dom ring!

2. My native country, thee
   Land of the noble free,
   Thy name I love;
   I love thy rocks and rills,
   Thy woods and templed hills,
   My heart with rapture thrills
   Like that above.

3. Let music swell the breeze,
   And ring from all the trees
   Sweet Freedom's song;
   Let mortal tongues awake,
   Let all that breathe partake,
   Let rocks their silence break,
   The sound prolong.

4. Our father's God! to Thee,
   Author of liberty,
   To Thee we sing;
   Long may our land be bright
   With freedom's holy light;
   Protect us by Thy might,
   Great God, our King!

AMERICA, THE BEAUTIFUL

Words and Music by
Katherine Lee Bates and Samuel A. Ward

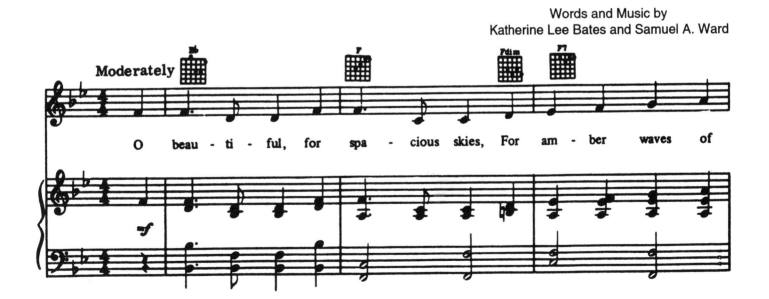

O beau - ti - ful, for spa - cious skies, For am - ber waves of

American Patrol

Music by
F. W. Meacham

Moderate March tempo

AMERICA, I LOVE YOU

Words by Edgar Leslie
Music by Archie Gottler

Anchors Aweigh

Words and Music by
Captain Alfred H. Miles, USN and Charles A. Zimmermann

Marcato moderato ma con spirito

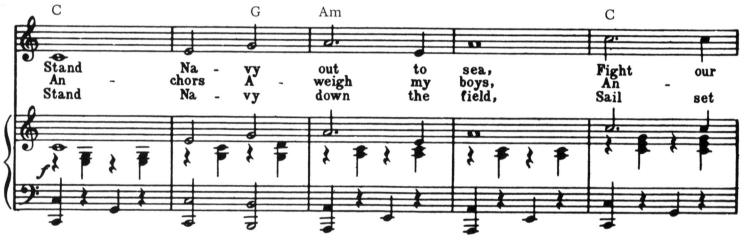

Are You From Dixie?

Words by Jack Yellen
Music by George L. Cobb

Beautiful Ohio

Words by Ballard MacDonald
Music by Mary Earl

Arkansas Traveler

Southern American Folksong

Hoe-down

Battle Cry of Freedom

Words and Music by
George F. Root

Chorus

The Un - ion for - ev - er, Hur - rah, boys, Hur-rah!

Down with the trai-tor, Up with the star; While we ral - ly round the flag, boys,

Ral - ly once a-gain, Shout - ing the bat - tle cry of Free - dom. Free - dom.

2.
We are springing to the call
Of our brothers gone before,
   Shouting the battle cry of Freedom,
And we'll fill the vacant ranks
With a million Free men more,
   Shouting the battle cry of Freedom.

Chorus

3.
We will welcome to our numbers
The loyal, true and brave,
   Shouting the battle cry of Freedom,
And although he may be poor
He shall never be a slave,
   Shouting the battle cry of Freedom.

Chorus

4.
So we're springing to the call
From the East and from the West,
   Shouting the battle cry of Freedom,
And we'll hurl the rebel crew
From the land we love the best,
   Shouting the battle cry of Freedom.

Chorus

Battle Hymn of the Republic

Words by Julia Ward Howe
Music by William Steffe

Bell Bottom Trousers

THE BONNIE BLUE FLAG

Words and Music by
Harry MacCarthy

rah for the Bon-nie Blue Flag, that bears a Sin-gle Star!

Chorus

Hur - rah! Hur - rah! for South-ern rights hur - rah! Hur -

rah! for the Bon-nie Blue Flag that bears a Sin-gle Star. 2. As Star.

2.

As long as the Union was faithful to her trust,
Like friends and brethren kind were we, and just;
But now, when Northern treachery attempts our rights to mar,
We hoist on high the Bonnie Blue Flag that bears a single star.

Chorus: Hurrah, hurrah, etc.

3.

First gallant South Carolina nobly made the stand,
Then came Alabama and took her by the hand;
Next, quickly, Mississippi, Georgia, and Florida,
All raised on high the Bonnie Blue Flag that bears a single star.

Chorus: Hurrah, hurrah, etc.

Boys, Keep Your Powder Dry

FOR YOUR COUNTRY AND MY COUNTRY

Words and Music by
Irving Berlin

The Caissons Go Rolling Along

Words and Music by
E. L. Gruber

O - ver hill, o - ver dale, as we hit the dust - y trail, And those cais - sons go roll - ing a - long.

COLUMBIA, THE GEM OF THE OCEAN

Words and Music by
Thomas A. Becket
and David T. Shaw

O, Co - lum - bia! the gem of the o - cean, The home of the brave___ and the free,___ The shrine of each pa - triot's de - vo - tion, A world___ of - fers hom - age to thee. Thy___ man - dates make he - roes as - sem - ble When___ Lib - er - ty's form___ stands in

EL CAPITAN

Music by
John Philip Sousa

FLAG SONG

God Bless Our Native Land

GOD OF OUR FATHERS

Words and Music by DANIEL C. ROBERTS
and GEORGE WARREN

HAIL, COLUMBIA

Words by Joseph Hopkinson
Music by Philip Phile

in - de - pen-dence be— our boast, Ev - er mind-ful what it cost,
of - f'ring peace, sin - cere and just, In heav'n we place a man - ly trust, That

Ev - er— grate-ful for— the— prize, Let its al - tar reach the skies.
truth and— jus - tice may— pre-vail, And ev - 'ry scheme of bond - age fail.

Chorus

Firm, u - nit - ed let— us— be, Ral - 'ying round our lib - er - ty,

As a band of_ broth-ers_join'd, Peace_ and_safe-ty we shall find.

3. Sound, sound the trump of fame,
Let Washington's great fame
Ring through the world with loud applause,
Ring through the world with loud applause,
Let ev'ry chime to freedom dear,
Listen with a joyful ear,
With equal skill, with God-like pow'r
He governs in the fearful hour
Of horrid war, or guides with ease
The happier time of honest peace.
Chorus

4. Beloved the chief who now commands,
Once more to serve his country stands,
The rock on which the storm will beat,
The rock on which the storm will beat.
But arm'd in virtue firm and true,
His hopes are fixed on Heav'n and you,
When hope was sinking in dismay,
When glooms obscured Columbia's day,
His steady mind from changes free
Resolv'd on Death or Liberty.
Chorus

CHORUS

Firm united let us be,
Ral'ying round our liberty,
As a band of brothers joined,
Peace and safety we shall find.

Liberty Bell March

Music by
John Philip Sousa

Quick march

Hail To The Chief

Words by Thomas Elli
Music by James Sanderson

(Back Home Again In)
INDIANA

Words by Ballard MacDonald
Music by James F. Hanley

THE LIBERTY SONG

Words by John Dickinson
Music by William Boyce

1. Come, join hand in hand, brave A - mer - i - cans all, And
2. Our wor - thy fore - fa - thers, let's give them a cheer, To

rouse your bold hearts at fair Lib - er - ty's call; No tyr - an - nous acts shall sup -
cli - mates un - known did cou - ra - geous - ly steer; Thro' o - ceans to des - erts for

press your just claim, Or stain with dis - hon - or A - mer - i - ca's name.
Free - dom they came, And dy - ing, be - queath'd us their free - dom and fame. In —

Chorus

3. The tree their own hands had to Liberty rear'd,
They lived to behold growing strong and revered;
With transport they cried, "Now our wishes we gain,
For our children shall gather the fruits of our pain."
Chorus

4. Then join hand in hand, brave Americans all,
By uniting we stand, by dividing we fall;
In so righteous a cause let us hope to succeed,
For heaven approves of each generous deed.
Chorus

CHORUS

In Freedom we're born and in Freedom we'll live.
Our purses are ready,
Steady, friends, steady;
Not as slaves, but as Freemen our money we'll give.

THE MARINES HYMN

Words and Music by
L. Z. Phillips

MEET ME IN ST. LOUIS, LOUIS

FROM "MEET ME IN ST. LOUIS"

Words by ANDREW B. STERLING
Music by KERRY MILLS

MARYLAND, MY MARYLAND

Words and Music by
James Ryder Randall

be the bat - tle queen of yore, Ma - ry-land, my Ma - ry-land! 2.Hark Ma - ry-land!

2.
Hark to an exiled son's appeal,
  Maryland, my Maryland!
My mother State, to thee I kneel,
  Maryland, my Maryland!
For life or death, for woe or weal,
Thy peerless chivalry reveal,
And gird they beauteous limbs with steel,
  Maryland, my Maryland!

3.
Thou wilt not cower in the dust,
  Maryland, my Maryland!
Thy beaming sword shall never rust,
  Maryland, my Maryland!
Remember Carroll's sacred trust.
Remember Howard's warlike thrust,
And all thy slumberers with the just,
  Maryland, my Maryland!

4.
Come! 'tis the red dawn of the day,
  Maryland, my Maryland!
Come with thy panoplied array,
  Maryland, my Maryland!
With Ringgold's spirit for the fray,
With Watson's blood at Monterey,
With fearless Lowe and dashing May,
  Maryland, my Maryland!

5.
Dear mother, burst the tyrant's chain,
  Maryland, my Maryland!
Virginia should not call in vain,
  Maryland, my Maryland!
She meets her sisters on the plain,
"Sic semper!" 'tis the proud refrain
That baffles minions back amain,
  Maryland, my Maryland!
Arise in majesty again,
  Maryland, my Maryland!

6.
Come! for thy shield is brighter and strong,
  Maryland, my Maryland!
Come! for thy dalliance does thee wrong,
  Maryland, my Maryland!
Come to thine own heroic throng,
Stalking with liberty along,
And chant thy dauntless slogan-song,
  Maryland, my Maryland!

7.
I see the blush upon thy cheek,
  Maryland, my Maryland!
But thou wast ever bravely meek,
  Maryland, my Maryland!
But lo! there surges forth a shriek,
From hill to hill, from creek to creek,
Potomac calls to Chesapeake,
  Maryland, my Maryland!

8.
Thou wilt not yield the vandal toll,
  Maryland, my Maryland!
Thou wilt not crook to his control,
  Maryland, my Maryland!
Better the fire upon the roll,
Better the shot, the blade, the bowl,
Than crucifixion of the soul,
  Maryland, my Maryland!

9.
I hear the distant thunder-bum,
  Maryland, my Maryland!
The "Old Line's" bugle, fife, and drum,
  Maryland, my Maryland!
She is not dead, nor deaf, nor dumb;
Huzza! she spurns the Northern scum —
She breathes! She burns! She'll come! She'll come!
  Maryland, my Maryland

The Missouri Waltz

Words by J. R. Shannon
Music by John Vallentine Eppel

Hush - a - bye, ma ba - by, slum - ber - time is com - in' soon; Rest yo' head up-

on my breast while Mom - my hums a tune; The sand - man is call - in' where

shad - ows are fall - in', While the soft breez - es sigh as in days long gone by.

My Old Kentucky Home

Words and Music by
STEPHEN C. FOSTER

The sun shines bright in the old Ken-tuck-y home; 'tis sum-mer, the dark-ies are
hunt no more for the pos-sum and the coon on the mead-ow, the hill and the
head must bow and the back will have to bend wher-ev-er the dark-ey may

gay. The corn top's ripe and the mead-ow's in the bloom, while the
shore. They sing no more by the glim-mer of the moon on the
go. A few more days and the trou-ble all will end in the

The Navy Hymn

Words by Rev. William Whiting
Music by Rev. John B. Dykes

Over There

Word and Music by
George M. Cohan

Oh! How I Hate to Get Up in the Morning

Words and Music by
Irving Berlin

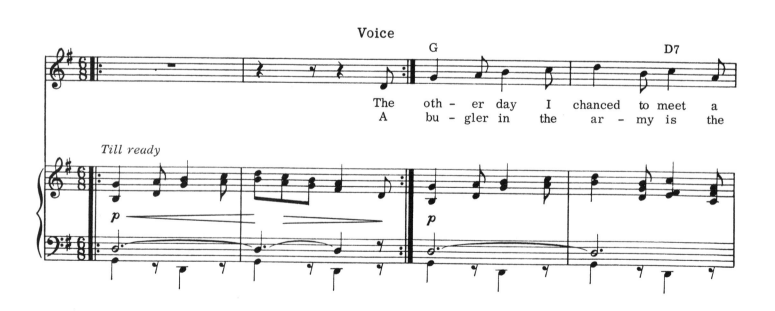

Chorus

ON WISCONSIN!

Words by CARL BECK
Music by W.T. PURDY

Semper Fidelis

Marcato Allegro

Music by
John Philip Sousa

Song of Islands

Moderately, in a flowing style

Words and Music by
Charles E. King

The Star Spangled Banner

Words and Music by
Francis Scott Key and John Stafford Smith

With Spirit

1. O_____ say, can you see, by the dawn's ear - ly
2. On the shore, dim - ly seen seen thro' the mists of the
3. O_____ thus be it ev - er when free - men shall

light, What so proud - ly we hailed at the twi - light's last
deep, Where the foe's haugh - ty host in dread si - lence re -
stand Be - tween their loved homes and the war's des - o -

gleam - ing? Whose broad stripes and bright stars, thro' the
pos - es, What is that which the breeze, o'er the
la - tion! Blest with vic - t'ry and peace, may the

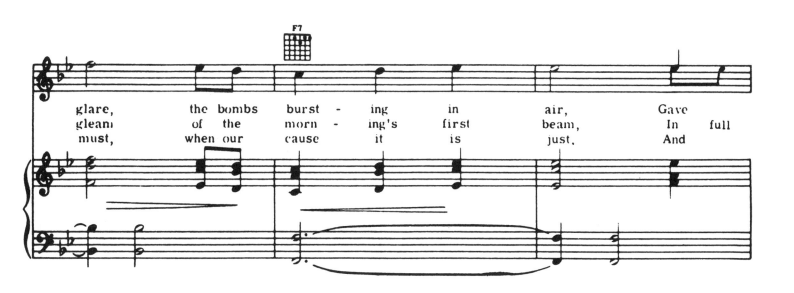

THE WASHINGTON POST MARCH

Bright march

Music by
John Philip Sousa

THE STARS AND STRIPES FOREVER

Music by
John Philip Sousa

With Spirit

Take Me Out to the Ball Game

Words by Jack Norworth
Music by Albert Von Tilzer

TRAMP! TRAMP! TRAMP!

Words and Music by
George F. Root

2.

In the battle front we stood
When their fiercest charge they made,
And they swept us off a hundred men or more;
But before we reach'd their lines
They were beaten back dismayed,
And we heard the cry of vict'ry o'er and o'er.

Chorus: Tramp, tramp, tramp, etc.

3.

So within the prison cell,
We are waiting for the day
That shall come to open wide the iron door;
And the hollow eye grows bright,
And the poor heart almost gay,
As we think of seeing home and friends once more.

Chorus: Tramp, tramp, tramp, etc.

Under the Double Eagle

Music by
Josef Wagner

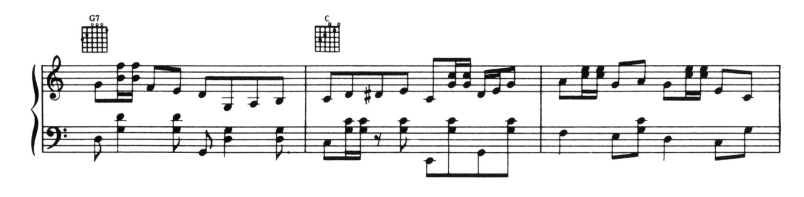

WHEN JOHNNY COMES MARCHING HOME

Yankee Doodle Dandy

Words and Music by
George M. Cohan

THE YELLOW ROSE OF TEXAS

1. There's a yel-low rose in Tex-as I'm go-ing there to see, no oth-er fel-low
(2. Where the) Ri-o Grande is flow-ing, Where stars are shin-ing bright, we walked a-long the
(3. Oh, I'm) go-ing back to find her, my heart is full of woe, We'll sing the songs to-

knows her, No-bod-y, on-ly me. She cried so, when I left her, it
riv-er, on a qui-et sum-mer night. She said if you re-mem-ber, we
geth-er, we sang so long a-go. I'll pick the ban-jo gai-ly, and

like to broke her heart; and if we ev-er meet a-gain, we nev-er more shall part.
part-ed long a-go, you prom-ised to come back a-gain, and nev-er leave me so.
sing the songs of yore, THE YEL-LOW ROSE OF TEX-AS, she'll be mine for-ev-er more.

YOU'RE A GRAND OLD FLAG

Words and Music by
George M. Cohan

Yankee Doodle

Traditional